KINGDOM WEALTH 101

The Generation Of The Upright Shall Be Blessed!

Paula Matthews

SL
Spirit & Life Publications[SM]
Atlanta

KINGDOM WEALTH 101

The Generation Of The Upright Shall Be Blessed!

Spirit & Life Publications℠
www.spiritandlifepublications.com
Atlanta

ISBN-13: 978-1-7357642-6-9
Printed in the United States

Author's Note

"Wealth & Dominion"

God gave me this book on Kingdom Wealth to share with others. This is not a book about money. Although it may mention God's purpose for money, this book introduces God's plan for earthly dominion.

We are in a season in which God is reclaiming the earth for His Purpose. He is taking back the earth, and the fulness thereof; the world and they that dwell therein (Psalm 24:1). The people, and the wealth, it all belongs to God. The last bastion of strength that the enemy refuses to relinquish, is the wealth of the world.

Therefore, this book is about the increase of God's Kingdom and His Peace throughout the world, to order it, and to establish it with judgment and with justice forever. The zeal of the Lord of hosts will perform this (Isaiah 9:7). This is not a work of man. This is a supernatural move of God upon the earth!

PROPHETIC WORD
Of The Lord

"Those Who Mocked
The Prosperity Message
Will Soon
Wish That They Had Listened.

They Will See It, But Not Taste It.

They Will Be Devastated
By What Is Coming To America."

This book comes with a strong warning from the Lord. There have been many who have spoken against the prosperity of God's people. They have mocked the so called "prosperity preachers" and the message God gave them to preach. Even as I write, there is a scripture coming up in my spirit, Hosea 4:6. God says by the mouth of the prophet, *"My people are destroyed for lack of knowledge."* Most people stop reading there, but let's continue with what God said. *"My people are destroyed for lack of knowledge: Because thou hast rejected knowledge . . ."* STOP!

God said His people are destroyed for lack of knowledge, but the truth of this lack comes to light. It's not because knowledge was not available. It's because they rejected the knowledge that was given to them. I'm hearing in my spirit that this scripture is also true concerning the knowledge of God's will to prosper His people. Because the knowledge of prosperity, or ***"the prosperity message"*** was rejected, God's people are destroyed, cut off from the Blessing God has for them. Please understand that knowledge was made available, but it was initially rejected by church leaders. In the prophetic word, the Lord not only said that

"The prosperity message" was rejected, but that it was ***"mocked."*** It is one thing to reject a message, but a more severe thing to mock the word of the Lord that you do not understand. I caution you not to do the same with this book. I am not writing because I desired to write another book. No! I am writing because God commanded me to write. He wants ***"the prosperity message revisited in truth."*** Why? That answer also lies within the prophetic word (warning) from the Lord. He said that the mockers of ***"the prosperity message . . . will be devastated by what is coming to America."*** This warning is to clergy and laymen alike. God says that these mockers ***"will wish that they had listened."*** Something is ***"coming to America"*** that will leave mockers ***"devastated."*** These are God's words, not mine. Even so, the Spirit of God is alerting me to know that the season is now.

When the Lord first gave me this word, He took me to II Kings 6:25. This was time of *"great famine"* in Samaria after they were besieged by the Syrians. God put a word in the mouth of the Prophet Elisha, announcing the end of the famine. *"Then Elisha said, Hear ye the word of the LORD; Thus saith the LORD, To morrow about this time [shall] a measure of fine flour [be sold] for a shekel, and two measures of barley for a shekel, in the gate of Samaria."* In this midst of this *"great famine,"* there was a mocker in the land who spoke against the word of the Lord that was spoken by Elisha. *"Then a lord on whose hand the king leaned answered the man of God, and said, Behold, [if] the LORD would make windows in heaven, might this thing be? And he [Elisha] said, Behold, thou shalt see [it] with thine eyes, but shalt not eat thereof* (II Kings 7:1-2)."

The famine ended exactly as Elisha had prophesied. The lord who mocked the prophet fell and was trampled to death as the people stampeded out of the city to spoil the Syrian tents. That mocker heard the word of the Lord. He also saw it come to pass, but his mockery brought him to his death. The Lord said to me, ***"those who mocked the prosperity message will soon wish that they had listened. They will see it, but not taste it. They will be devastated by what is coming to America."*** Is a famine coming to America? God didn't specify, but He is encouraging His people to heed this word about Kingdom Wealth. This book will impart understanding to those who want to survive what is coming to America in these last days.

"So shall My Word be
That goeth forth out of My Mouth:
It shall not return unto Me void,
But it shall accomplish
That which I Please,
And it shall
Prosper [in the thing]
Whereto I sent it."

Isaiah 55:11

Prosperity Defined

Now, that we have heard the warning, we will embark upon the truth. What is God's definition of prosperity? Many have rejected the so called ***"prosperity message"*** because they have never heard the real gospel of the Kingdom. We will discuss that next, however before we talk about the Kingdom we need to define *prosperity*. Many have taught that *prosperity* was about money. That's an American interpretation of *prosperity* because we are a country that is mammon or money centered. We are amongst those who worship the almighty dollar instead of the Almighty God. Therefore, our interpretation of *prosperity* is tainted.

God took me from the Baptist church and put me in the Word of Faith movement where faith and *prosperity* were often the focus. However, the definition I received concerning *prosperity* came directly from the Lord. Money was never the focus of my life, but my concept of ministry was from the belief that God had no interest in money. That is what I always thought; that God was more interested in our spiritual development than our having money. I heard so much talk from people about money, houses, cars, and material things, that it disturbed me. Rather than objecting to what they were saying, I went to God for clarification. He had never spoken to me about material things back then. My pastor never spoke about obtaining material things, but other ministers did. God spoke to me about building schools and orphanages around the world. When I ask how all of this would be done, it was then that God began teaching me about Kingdom Wealth strategies. It was always about money with a **"Kingdom Mission."**

I asked God to clarify the Kingdom definition of *prosperity*. He said, ***"Prosperity is the word manifested in your divine destiny."*** This comes from Isaiah 55:10-11. *"For as the rain cometh down, and the snow from heaven, and returneth not thither, but watereth the earth, and maketh it bring forth and bud, that it may give seed to the sower, and bread to the eater: So shall my word be that goeth forth out of my mouth: it shall not return unto me void, but it shall accomplish that which I please, and it shall prosper [in the thing] whereto I sent it."* When the word of God for your life and destiny comes to pass, this is the definition of *prosperity*. Also notice that this prosperity is two-fold. It is for seed to sow (give) and for us to eat (consume). The first emphasis should be on giving to the **"Kingdom Mission."** The issue has been that people have gotten ***"mixed messages"*** concerning *prosperity.* Pastors talking about owning a jet because another preacher has one, may send a message of greed. But, when the Lord tells me that in order to fulfill my assignment, that I need ***"a fleet"*** of jets, then that's a ***"Kingdom need."*** Preachers "believing God" for millions of dollars to build a church, may seem like greed to a person with a lesser vision from God. The Lord gave me a project and chastised me saying that my multi-billion dollar ***"budgets were too low."*** When I threw down my pencil and asked, "Just how much money do I need to successfully complete this project?" The Lord responded, ***"trillions."*** That's not greed. For me, that's a ***"Kingdom need."***

This is why God gave me this book to write on Kingdom Wealth. It's bigger than we think. It's bigger than our wants and desires. As the Lord told me, this is about replacing and ***"undergirding"*** the financial health of nations. This is the Blessing of Abraham in our day. *"And thou shalt lend unto many nations, and thou shalt not borrow* (Deuteronomy 28:12)." God spoke to me about His people being able to ***"bail out***

nations." It's been twenty years since the Lord began showing me a series of events that would shake the world economy. Prosperity is more serious than buying a big house or a fancy car. God said to me, ***"My people will need food."*** God is preparing for His people to take on the welfare of the nations. Back then the only thing I knew that could cause such lack and devastation in the world was war. God spoke to me about war coming to the shores of America. What I didn't see back then, was a pandemic causing nations to scramble in order to survive. There are shortages of necessities and no workers to fulfill the jobs. If Christians don't quickly understand God's Kingdom Wealth and economy, they will not survive these end times.

It's time to get into the word of God and gain essential knowledge of God's Kingdom and His way of doing things. The ways of the world have come to an end. World leaders have no answers. Consequently, God's Kingdom is the world's only hope. ***"The works of man are over. It's My Time,"*** **says God.** Without a vision and plan from God, the people of earth would surely perish. Thank God for the remnant amongst us who have been anointed and appointed for this Wealth assignment. They have been busy preparing ***"an ark"*** of protection from the perils of these last days. God's Kingdom is our only refuge from what is coming upon the earth. Therefore, God has urged me by His Spirit to ***"finish the book"*** on Kingdom Wealth. This is not a doom and gloom story, nor is it a simple story about money coming to God's people. This is a story about God Blessing His people and demonstrating His love and compassion for all humanity. *"And it shall be to me a name of joy, a praise and an honour before all the nations of the earth, which shall hear all the good that I do unto them: and they shall fear and tremble for all the goodness and for all the prosperity that I procure unto it* (Jeremiah 33:9)."

In these last days, prophetic voices will proclaim the Father's will to prosper His people in the midst of worldwide famine and chaos. God said that ***"these signs*** **[Wealth]** ***shall follow those who believe in these last days before Jesus returns."*** This word about Kingdom Wealth will not return to the Father void. It shall accomplish what God pleases and it shall prosper in the true gospel of the Kingdom being preached and demonstrated worldwide. In Jesus' Name.

"The Lord
Is
A Man Of War."

Exodus 15:3

The Gospel Of The Kingdom Explained

Before one can understand Kingdom Wealth, he or she must understand the truth about God's earthly Kingdom. It's more than God's way of operating in this earth. The world is God's domain, His territory that He created from the very beginning, before time, for the habitation of His sons and daughters (Genesis 1,2,3). Psalm 24:1 also confirms that "*The earth <u>is</u> the Lord's and the fulness thereof, the world, and they that dwell therein.*" Let's get this one thing straight right here and now. The earth, its inhabitants, and all its possessions belong to God. They were His from the beginning and when it is all said and done, EVERY ONE <u>and</u> EVERY THING on earth will be restored back into the Father's Hands. Restoration <u>is</u> the end time plan of God for the entire planet.

Jesus came, not to take us to Heaven, but to take back the Earth <u>for</u> Heaven's sake. He came to restore back to the Father, EVERY THING that Adam lost, not just the garden of Eden, but also the power and earthly dominion God had given him under the Blessing. When Adam sinned, the Blessing was replaced by the curse. All of mankind was doomed to live in the curse, estranged from the One who created them, and far from the Blessing that was to be upon their lives for all eternity. If Adam had never sinned, this earth would have been filled with righteous men and women communing with the Father. We would have been living as heirs of this world, performing God's will throughout the earth for all generations. This was the ETERNAL LIFE God had in mind for every human born into this planet. Sin changed the game plan, but God never changed His mind about his human creation.

The gospel of Jesus Christ was never about us going to Heaven. It was always about God's people taking dominion over the earth, for His Kingdom. Jesus taught only about the Kingdom. Then He demonstrated the power of the Kingdom when He healed the sick and raised the dead. The gospel was always about restoring God's supernatural power to ***"restore and replenish"*** the earth under the Blessing. Restoration will continue to be God's plan for the earth until every prophetic word is fulfilled. That includes every prophetic word in the Bible, and those that have been spoken over our lives by the Holy Spirit.

These prophetic words are not for Heaven. They were spoken to bring about God's will in this earth. They are sent by God to guide us into all truth (John 16:13) until Jesus comes.

God gave this planet as an inheritance to His children (Psalm 2:8). When God created mankind He Blessed us and empowered us to have dominion in this earth. "*And God blessed them, and God said unto them, Be fruitful, and multiply, and replenish the earth, and subdue it: and have dominion* (Genesis 1:28)." Jesus came to restore the dominion of the Blessing back to those who would obey God.

We have been empowered to dominate over every evil in the earth. The devil knows it all too well. That is why he is busy sending plagues and threatening the welfare of all humanity. Just sit tight and watch what God unveils in these last days. A mighty army is about to embark upon the scene, with all the power of Heaven backing them. They will be taking down kingdoms and reclaiming territories for Almighty God. This is a revelation that came straight out of Heaven, when I was taken into the **Lord's War Room**. Before going to the War Room, I was taken to the **Lord's Armory** where I saw the weapons that were available for God's people here on the earth. I saw weapons far more advanced than our modern technology. All those teachings about Christians wearing Roman armor was just an example the Apostle Paul used for the people of His day (Ephesians 6:10-18). They don't apply to us. The armor we have at our disposal today is light years ahead of what men could ever conceive. The Lord has provided more than enough weaponry for us to take down the enemy. We need only to listen to His Spirit and obey His instructions.

Kingdom Wealth is not about money. It's about a worldwide take over! The Lord is ***"Taking Back"*** the earth, its people and possessions for His glory. Salvation was never about Heaven. It was always about restoring ***"Worldwide Dominion,"*** for God's Kingdom. The Lord spoke to me about WAR! It is from this context that He taught me about the purpose for Kingdom Wealth.

The Lord's War Room

I will never forget going to Heaven and being escorted into the Lord's War Room by the Lord Himself. This was not a sightseeing trip to Heaven. What I didn't know at the time was that the Lord was about to commission me for a high level end time global mission. King Jesus was about to show me in vivid detail, what must be done before He returns to the earth.

I recall walking into the large room where there was a large table in the center. On the surface of that table was a map of the world. The Lord said that this map represented the world under Satan's captivity after Adam sinned. The world fell under enemy occupation after Adam lost his place as ruler of this earth. It was then that the people and possessions of earth were overtaken by satanic rule, until Jesus came.

When Jesus gave His life on the cross, He became the ransom for all mankind (I Timothy 2:6). I saw the legal document stating that the earth and all its people and possessions were legally given back to God. That document certified in writing that Jesus had bought back the entire earth for God's Kingdom. The Lord explained how everything that was restored has been placed in receivership for the Body of Christ to claim and manage until Jesus comes back to reign on earth.

I was unfamiliar with how a receivership works. So I had to do some research. In it's simplest terms, a legal receivership is when a court appoints a person to care for the property of another. The Court of Heaven gave the Body of Christ ***"legal receivership."*** We are responsible to recover, manage, and oversee everything that belongs to God in this earth. The Bible calls it being a *"steward."* A steward has responsibilities over his or her master's goods and must be found faithful if they want to remain in their Lord's good graces. Not only are we stewards of God's earth, we are also *"stewards of the mysteries of God* (I Corinthians 4:1-2)." This book unfolds such mysteries.

Whatever God reveals by His Spirit is to help us obtain our earthly inheritances. As the Bible says, *"The secret things belong unto the Lord our God; but those things which are revealed belong unto us and to our children for ever, that we may do all the word of this law* (Deuteronomy 29:29)." When the Lord took me to Heaven and revealed His military strategy for earth, I guarded every word with my life. I never revealed anything until **He said** it was time. There are still many things that I have not been allowed to reveal, but this word about Kingdom Wealth, God has urged to me release now. Although I have written about Covenant Wealth in the past, and I have told of my War Room visit many times, the Spirit of God is urging me to release this entire message for such a time as this. The world is about to experience some "perilous times" and we the people of God must be prepared to be good stewards of God's earth.

While in the War Room, the Lord drew my attention to another map of the world that was hanging on the wall. It was the legal document showing the earth and its territories as they had been restored to God. To my surprise, everything on that map had a family name attached to it. Immediately I saw holdings with my name on them in various places in the world. There were even inventions and products this world has never seen. They all had the names of God's people attached to them. Everything had names on it, including industries and governments around the world. It all belonged to God's children according to that legal document. The Bible says, "*The heaven, even the heavens, are the LORD'S: but the earth hath he given to the children of men* (Psalm 115:16)." That map was spiritual evidence that everything in earth was created for God's family. I saw it with my own eyes. I could never deny what the Lord showed me in that War Room. It was astonishing! I knew what the Bible said, but it was still a shock to see with my own eyes that indeed God's kids were given dominion over everything in this earth. It's ours!

Going back to the beginning, we know that God created us in his image and likeness and gave us dominion (Genesis 1:26-28). THE PLAN of God was for mankind to walk in HIS WILL, and not in our own. Just imagine how life would have been for us, had Adam never sinned. That legal document in Heaven stated that mankind had been redeemed back to *"sinless"* status. Jesus paid the price in full. Unfortunately, not everyone knows about this legal (covenant) arrangement between God and Jesus. However, for everyone who receives Jesus Christ as Lord, God treats them as though sin had never existed. This *"sinless"* status entitles them to an earthly inheritance from the Father. Although many are saved, very few are expecting an inheritance on this earth. The reason is quite simple. Many Christians have the belief that God does not want us to have money or nice things in this earth. Let me take a moment to confront this issue. This is not another ***"mixed message."*** Jesus taught, *"But lay up for yourselves treasures in heaven, where neither moth nor rust doth corrupt, and where thieves do not break through nor steal: For where your treasure is, there will your heart be also* (Matthew 6:20-21)." This is an issue of the heart. What do you treasure God or things? God will give you earthly treasures when you *"seek those things which are above"* where Christ sits (Colossians 3:1). Here is an example.

Solomon is known as the richest king that ever lived. The Bible says that God appeared to Solomon in a dream at night saying (I Kings 3:5-13), *"Ask what I shall give thee?"* The king responded, *"Give therefore thy servant an understanding heart to judge thy people, that I may discern between good and bad: for who is able to judge this thy so great a people?"* The Bible says that it pleased God that Solomon asked this thing. Here is how God responded to the king. This should give you insight to why God made Solomon rich. God said, *"Behold, I have done according to thy words . . . And I have also given thee that which thou hast not asked, both riches, and honour: so that there shall not be any among the kings like unto thee all thy days.*" Solomon put God's Kingdom agenda first and God gave the king wealth and riches that he didn't ask for. *"But seek ye first the kingdom of God, and his righteousness, and all these things shall be added unto you* (Matthew 6:33)." Wealth is part of our earthly inheritance as sons and daughters of God.

The Bible says that we have an inheritance, *"incorruptible, and undefiled, and that fadeth not away, reserved in heaven for you who are kept by the power of God through faith unto salvation ready to be revealed in the last time* (I Peter 1:4-5)." More about our salvation is being revealed in these last days. Our earthly inheritance is reserved for us in Heaven, but a portion has been made available to us in this earth. In fact, the Holy Spirit is the *"earnest"* deposit of that inheritance (Ephesians 1:14). The remainder we will receive indeed *"in the last time."* This is a covenant promise. The Holy Spirit is ***"the executor of the covenant."*** He will reveal to us what is available in our earthly inheritance. He will also give instructions as to how to receive that inheritance.

Don't get hung up on the talk about money, wealth or inheritance. Take a moment to think about what the Bible says that Jesus did for humanity. He paid the *ransom* with His life. What happens if someone is held for a ransom, and that ransom is paid? The person would be returned to his or her original familial position. Right? Well, that is what salvation affords every believer. We were reconciled back to our Father, to the position He predestined for us before the foundation of the world.

Consider this. Adam sinned and we were all held hostage by the kingdom of darkness. Our earthly inheritances were stolen. Salvation released us from the power of darkness and translated us into God's Kingdom where we were restored back to our rightful positions in Christ. Again, if Adam had never sinned, we would have been living in the luxurious abundance and splendor as sons and daughters of God. It would have been truly "days of heaven upon the earth." This was, and continues to be the inheritance God has for each of us. The whole purpose of salvation is to bring us back into the glory of our Father's House, just like what happened in the parable about the prodigal son.

The prodigal son demanded that his father give him his inheritance. After receiving from his father, he left home. According to the Bible *"he wasted his substance with riotous living* (Luke 15:13)." This young man squandered his wealth and found himself in famine, wanting to eat with the pigs. The Bible says that *"he came to himself"* and realized that his father's servants had more than enough to eat. He went home, *"no more worthy"* to be called a son, but desiring to be a hired servant. The father did not want another servant, he celebrated the restoration of his son with the *"best"* of everything. *"For this my son was dead, and is alive again; he was lost, and is found* (Luke 15:24)."

This is a message about ***"provision,"*** for had not the young man lost everything and had no way to feed himself, he probably would have never returned to his father's house. It was his desperate state that brought him to repentance, and so it is with most of us. This book is about Kingdom Wealth. It's not so much about money as it is about God's supernatural provision for these last days. These are basic concepts that should help one understand how salvation was never meant to be without ***"financial reparations," or "recompense."***

Let's stay in that legal context for a moment. One would never petition a court of law and not expect to be compensated for a wrong that had been suffered. Yet, Jesus went to the Court of Heaven and won the battle against the evil one who held the world captive in lies and deception. Jesus ***"received restitution for all humanity."*** Where is that written in the Bible? Isaiah 53:11-12 tells how God was pleased with the suffering Jesus endured for us. "*Therefore will I* [God] *divide him a portion with the great, and he shall divide the spoil with the strong.*" Jesus entered into the "*strong man's house*" and spoiled his goods (Matthew 12:29).

The Apostle Paul summed up the purpose of salvation in a few simple words. "*To open their eyes, and to turn them from darkness to light, and from the power of Satan unto God, that they may receive forgiveness of sins, and inheritance among them which are sanctified by faith that is in me* (Acts 26:18)." We are saved and sanctified by faith, to receive "*the forgiveness of sins and inheritance.*" Shall we go a little deeper? Jesus restored back to us everything that Adam lost. What did He receive for us? Revelation 5:10 tells us what Jesus received after His sacrifice on that cross. "*Worthy is the Lamb that was slain to receive power, and riches, and wisdom, and strength, and honour, and glory, and blessing."* Jesus gave His life as a ransom on that cross, so that we could receive *"power, and riches, and wisdom, and strength, and honour, and glory, and blessing."* Jesus didn't need these things on earth. He had all of this and more when He was with the Father in Heaven. This is the spoil He divided among the strong. The Bible says that Jesus was rich, but He became poor for our sakes, that we *"through His poverty might be rich* (II Corinthians 8:9)."

Jesus made that devil pay for all that humanity had suffered. Compare our case with that of the prodigal son. He chose to leave his father's house and strike out on his own. Whereas we were born as sinners and ***"outcasts"*** not by choice, but because of Adam's sin. Now, here are the similarities with the prodigal. Although the prodigal humbled himself and desired to be a servant in his father's house, he was welcomed back home with open arms. He didn't come home to some low status of servitude. Neither did we. His father ran to his son and lavished him with the best of everything. That is how God wants to treat each of His children, if we would only let Him. God wants ***"to restore to each of us, what we would have had,***

if sin had never entered the earth." Too many Christians see themselves as lowly servants not deserving of any lavishment from the Father, but that is not how God sees us. He sees us exactly like that father did who received his prodigal back home again. God is a good Father. He desires to lavish His kids with the best of everything. After all, we are a Royal Family.

Even King Solomon made an observation he called *"an evil," "under the sun." "Folly is set in great dignity, and the rich sit in low place. I have seen servants upon horses, and princes walking as servants upon the earth.* (Ecclesiastes 10:5-7)." In other words, God's kids, the **real** royals in this world are walking as servants upon th earth and our Heavenly Father is not being glorified. We are not walking in the fullness of what Jesus paid for with His life. Now, some of you may say, "I don't need all of that." The prodigal didn't need lavishment either. All he wanted was food to eat, yet his father lavished his son with fine apparel and a fancy party. The father loved the boy that much. He was so overcome by the restoration of his son, that the father withheld no good thing from him. How much more would our Heavenly Father do the same for everyone who turns from sin and returns to Him?

I recall the first time the Lord came to me and asked, ***"What shall I do for you?"*** I told Him that He was all I needed and that He didn't have to give me anything. God the Father corrected me. He said, ***"I have to do this for you. It's My Word."*** All I could do was agree with God and receive. This was difficult at first. I had to learn how to receive from God. Later it occurred to me that God needed to ***"showcase"*** His goodness through my life. I knew He was good when He healed my body. I knew that God was good when He protected me from obvious danger. Yet, that was the first of many times that I would experience the goodness of God in prospering me materially.

Kingdom Wealth is not about us. It's about God's word. It has been hard for many to believe that God wants to give us good things in this life. Doesn't every good parent want do good for their children? God did it for the Jewish people all throughout the Bible. Abraham was rich. So were his sons Isaac and Jacob. We serve the same God. According to scripture, we who are in Christ are Abraham's seed and heirs to the same promise (Galatians 3:29). It's time we receive what is rightfully ours and let the world know that God is a good Father.

Speaking of the Jews. There was another thing that struck me about that map on the wall in the War Room. All those names on that map reminded me of those ancient Bible maps that showed how the land was divided among the twelve tribes of Israel. The Bible tells about the promised land of the Jews. The Lord showed me that everyone who comes into His family has an inheritance in the land. We all have a place on earth in which to dominate. The Lord explained that the entire earth was to be divided amongst all of God's children. All we need do is ask the Father to reveal what belongs to us. "*Ask of me, and I shall give [thee] the heathen [for] thine inheritance, and the uttermost parts of the earth [for] thy possession* (Psalm 2:8)."

Understand that there are those who teach that our Christian inheritance is only spirit. Not so! Abraham's inheritance was physical. As his seed, through Christ, we are heirs of the same promise. We also have a spiritual inheritance through Jesus Christ. Our inheritance is both physical and spiritual. Each of us has to seek first the Kingdom and let the Lord reveal what belongs to us.

We, the Church of Jesus Christ are called to go out into this world and recover everything (people and possessions) for the Kingdom! The Church is not the building, but the people of God, *the elect* (Matthew 24:31), those called to service in the Kingdom. According to the Lord, everything I saw on that wall map, has to be claimed before He can return to earth. We are to claim the land and occupy til He comes (Luke 19:13).

This is a Kingdom military occupation. We don't contend with men. We war against demonic forces of darkness that rule this world system. The world system is coming down. Our job as believers is to rescue the loss, give them refuge in the Kingdom and nourish them with love and compassion until the Savior, King Jesus arrives. Therefore, Kingdom Wealth is not about money. It's about God's Kingdom purpose in this earth.

Wealth With A Kingdom Purpose

The Lord sent me to Los Angeles in 1997. He said that everything that had been stolen in my life would be returned to me in that place [*restoration*]. After arriving in LA, there were prophets in the Church talking about ***God raising up Black millionaires and billionaires for the Kingdom***. There were ministers talking about how God was going to give them $50 million dollars for houses and limousines. God was not speaking to me about receiving millions of dollars, nor was He speaking to me about houses and limos.

The Lord talked to me about starting a publishing company. He also gave me my first book and began showing the many books that I would write in the future. He also talked to me about producing film and television programs for the Kingdom. I had worked in television and film. I had written scripts and produced a television program, but to write a book was very intimidating. In none of this could I see money. All I could see was WORK. Then one day, the Lord gave me a vision about a children's series that would begin as a book. Later it would launch into movies, games and toys. He said, ***"It will bring in millions upon millions of dollars. The people will not be able to get enough of it."*** My first response was, "What do you care about money?" That was the first thing out of my mouth. Why? Because I had been taught that God didn't care about us having money. The Lord didn't answer my question. He went on talking about this series being ***"supernatural."*** So, I asked, "Are they ready for the supernatural?" God responded, ***"They are hungry for the supernatural."***

A year or so later, God's word was confirmed. Television series and films about the supernatural had become popular in the United States. The people were very hungry for supernatural power. If they were ready for witchcraft, they may be ready to hear about God's supernatural power too. Still no more talk from God about money. Instead, He had me focusing on the purpose of the series. He kept me focused on the assignment. It was a concept and idea from the Father that would make multiplied millions of dollars and teach the nations about the supernatural power of His Kingdom.

Notice how it was not about the money. It was about the **"Kingdom Mission."** This was just one way, God will use to bring wealth back into the Kingdom. God has given His people instructions on how to build things for the Kingdom that will *"replenish"* whatever is lacking in the earth. Whether it is food shortage, or lack of education and training in an area, God has a plan available. Attached to that plan is the wealth necessary to execute the plan and purpose of God.

The Lord is also a genius at creating business in stagnant markets. Remember how Peter *"toiled all night"* and was unable to catch any fish (Luke 5:4-5). He was a fisherman by trade, but the industry dried up. Jesus came along with prophetic wisdom in the form of an instruction. He stepped into one of Peter's ships and said, *"Launch out into the deep, and let down your nets for a draught."* When Peter obeyed Jesus' word they caught so many fish that his net broke. Peter had to call his partners to help him. Imagine the wealth that came to that industry, all because Peter put aside his knowledge of the business and obeyed the word of the Lord. This impacted the economy of that entire village.

What happened to Peter could happen to any person who would inquire of the Lord about how to do business the Kingdom way. God knows all things. He is also a god of increase. The instructions He gives may not make sense to our human understanding, but it will always bring forth miraculous results when we obey Him. People will know that it was not human effort that brought forth the miraculous results. This sets the stage for the gospel to be preached as people begin to question how it was done.

This is how the gospel of the Kingdom was intended to be preached, with signs (miracles) following. This is why God desires that we would hear His voice and follow it. As we obey the word, it will cause miracles to break out in the sight of the world all around us. This is the *"light"* that the world is literally ***"dying"*** to see in our day. How can they see, if we don't obey? How can we obey if we don't hear the voice of the Lord? How can we hear, unless we set out hearts to seek Him in prayer? The world is waiting to see our good works, and they will glorify our Father who is in Heaven (Matthew 5:16). Kingdom Wealth glorifies God. Wealth is coming to those who want God to be glorified in the earth.

A great harvest of souls is about to transition into the Kingdom. Many of these souls who have great wealth will be so grateful to God for delivering them, that they will pour all they have into God's Kingdom. Not many are preaching about this aspect of the wealth transfer. Sinners will be repenting and bringing their wealth into the Kingdom. We've just assumed that wealth was being taken from the sinner and given to the righteous. Not necessarily so. Neither will wealth come to people just because they call themselves "righteous." God is a just god.

The Bible says, *"the wealth of the sinner is laid up for the just* (Proverbs 13:22)." The *"sinner"* in this scripture may also include those who call themselves Christians. Becoming a member of a local church body does not make you *"just."* You must have received Jesus Christ as your Lord and Savior. You must be converted. You must be one who walks by faith in what Jesus did on that cross. As the Bible says, *"The just shall live by faith* (Hebrews 10:38)." Without faith, we cannot please God (Hebrews 11:6). If God is not pleased with us, what purpose would it serve for Him to give us wealth? The wealth is for those who desire to obey God. It is for those who have the ***"heart of***

***the Father.*"** Many people want the wealth to spend on themselves. They have little or no understanding of God's purpose for money. This is especially true of Christians in America. We have a jaded view of money and its purpose. That's why people say that money is evil. Money is not evil. The Bible says that *"the love of money is the root of all evil* (I Timothy 6:10)." Christians don't love money. We love God. Therefore, a "true" believer who loves God, will do what God says with the money. It takes knowing the heart of the Father, if you want to handle Kingdom Wealth.

We also don't seek after money. We seek first the Kingdom (Matthew 6:33). We seek the Creator God, not the created things. When we worship Him alone, then all things that we need in this world will follow us. As it says in Deuteronomy 28:1-2, if we obey His Voice, all of the Blessings will come on us and overtake us. Some Christians are expecting that wealth will automatically come to them. No! That devil will not release a cent without a fierce battle. The economic system of America and that of the nations are failing. God has been warning for years that this would happen. We are about to see the wicked rich brought down and their property divided among the righteous sons and daughters of God (Acts 13:19). God said ***"it's time."*** The wealth in America has been ***"squandered and hoarded by a handful of rich men."*** Here is one of the prophecies God gave me concerning the Wealth and Power Transfer in America:

"I am God and will not be mocked by any man; no matter how much wisdom and wealth he has gained. It all belongs to Me, and I decide who has possession of the wealth. You evil rich men have brought this country to the ruin, but I have a people amongst you who have been given the plan to prosper America. I will take your wealth and give it to them. They have My heart for the people. They have My anointing to get My plan done in the earth."

"This is My Kingdom hour to demonstrate My goodness and mercy to all mankind, and it will be done in America whom I have chosen for this demonstration so that all men can see that I am God and I have always loved My human creation; and have only plans to do you good and not evil. I love you, come to Me and see the great and mighty plan I have for your lives."

Beloved, as true believers in Jesus Christ, when we take a stand according to the instructions of the Lord, the host of Heaven will shakedown the enemy until all things (including wealth) are restored back to us. Is there a Biblical precedent of such a wealth transfer? Yes. Every prophetic word (revelation) fulfills ***"legal principles stated in the Bible."*** There are many wealth transfers mentioned in the Bible, but the Lord keeps taking me back to what happened in Egypt, when He released His people from slavery. God's people plundered the wealth of that nation (Exodus 12:36). Let's be clear, God is not just taking us out of bondage. He is ***"recompensing"*** us for all we have suffered while in bondage. This is a wealth and power takeover. Are you ready to possess the land? Who will go for the God?

The Lord said that He has is a remnant in the earth who will D O M I N A T E for the Kingdom. The Lord said it is time for His sons and daughters to ***"Recover All!"*** This will indeed be the greatest wealth and power transfer the world has ever seen. There will be nothing lacking to us, neither small or great, neither sons nor daughters, neither spoil, nor anything that is rightfully ours. We will take back everything and make that thief pay back seven times what he stole (Proverbs 6:31). We have a commission from our Lord. Like David, we will go into the enemy camp and take back all that he stole from us. We will have recovered so much that we will be able to send a portion of the spoils to our partners and friends (I Samuel 30:19, 20, 26-31). With God's faith, we will *"pursue . . . overtake . . . and without fail, recover all."*

Faith is not for the weak. We have to be strong in the Lord. We must be bold to lay hold to what God says is ours. Our strength comes from what we believe. As Apostle Paul said, " *for I know whom I have believed, and am persuaded that he is able to keep that which I have committed unto him against that day* (II Timothy 1:12)." It's time to go and possess the land for God's Kingdom. ***"Is there not a cause?"***

"How long [are] ye slack to go to possess the land,
Which the LORD God of your fathers hath given you?"
Joshua 18:3

***"He answered
And said unto them,
Give ye them to eat."***

Mark 6:37

Kingdom Wealth At Work

In these last days, God is not giving His people wealth just to let it accumulate. No! He is redistributing the wealth so that it can be put to work for the good of the nations. Even as I write, it has been more than a year since a worldwide pandemic began. People are still sick and dying. Resources have been ***"siphoned off"*** and the governments of the world are shackling people with even more restrictions, even threatening job loss if they refuse to take a vaccine. Evil is ruling over the people of the world, simply because wicked men are controlling the money and power in this earth. This ***"siege of evil"*** is over for the people of God.

The Lord prepared my heart years ago to see such days. He said, ***"My people will need food."*** Some Christians will be looking for manna to fall from the sky. It could happen, but the reality is that God has been preparing His people by giving them plans for building ***"an ark"*** for these last days. That is what happened to me. I didn't ask for Jesus to do a miracle. No! He pretty much told me, "*Give ye them to eat* (Mark

6:37)." God gave me a plan to implement in times of trouble. Consider what it would take to supply food and water for an entire community in a typical emergency. It would take millions and billions of dollars. Even more would be required if you had to provide shelter or emergency rescue services. As the heirs of God we are expected to manage (steward) this earth. Wealth is needed to *adequately* steward what belongs to God. Even during the time of the 911 attacks on America, we witnessed many miracles in which food mysteriously appeared in cabinets. Money appeared in people's homes. The Hand of God protected us from danger. God will continue to do miracles as we obey His instructions. It's like Mother Mary told the servants when they ran out of wine at the wedding feast. "*Whatsoever he saith unto you, do it* (John 2:5)."

People need God's intervention in their lives. Kingdom Wealth involves more than money. It's supernatural provision. It's the power and the glory of God in operation to heal, deliver and set people free from all kinds of bondages in this earth. It's not all about money. It's about the ***"total wellbeing of human kind."*** The Kingdom of God is not about satisfying our own desires. It's about having God's righteousness, peace and joy that comes from the Holy Ghost (Romans 14:17). To be truly wealthy means to be at peace and one with Almighty God. It's the person identified in Psalm 112 who is Blessed because they fear God and love His commandments. It's the relationship with the Father that causes them to obtain wealth and righteousness. Wealth and riches are in their house. Their children are Blessed. They give generously to the poor. They handle their affairs with discretion. They trust the Lord. Their righteousness endures forever. They are honored and exalted. The wicked will see it and gnash with his teeth, but he can do nothing about. ***"God is unstoppable."***

Beloved, God is looking for ***"wealth carriers"*** for His Kingdom. He wants to showcase His wealth and power through you. This kind of wealth carries with it a powerful **"Kingdom Mission"** of destroying the works (plots, lies and deception) of the devil (I John 3:8). How will this work? Jesus demonstrated it for us in His ministry. He came to destroy the works of the devil. What works? Sickness, death, poverty, blindness, lameness, deafness, are works of the devil. These conditions are not from God. That devil is a liar and a thief. His wants to steal our health and our wealth, and put the blame on God. Religion may even try to convince you that God sent these things to teach us a lesson. Don't believe it! Throughout the Bible, God has always healed and delivered His people. "*He sent His word and healed them, and delivered them from their destructions* (Psalm 107:20)." God sent Jesus to take away our sins, our griefs and sorrows. That's why God made Him the Healer, "*And with His stripes we are healed* (Isaiah 53:4-5)." The Bible says that God anointed Jesus with the Holy Ghost and power, "*who went about doing good, and healing all that were oppressed of the devil; for God was with him* (Acts 10:38)."

God anoint us, His people, with the same Holy Ghost and power. He didn't anoint us just so that devil could continue destroying human lives. No! We are the LIGHT OF THE WORLD. We are God's Kingdom representatives, ambassadors for Christ (II Corinthians 5:20) in this earth. Consider this. What would Jesus do if He were walking this earth today? Now, go and do likewise, ye Christian. That's the great commission the Lord gave us. ***Go into all the sectors of the world and preach [and demonstrate] the power of the gospel of the Kingdom.*** How do we do this? What did He tell the disciples? "*Preach saying, the kingdom of heaven is at hand. Heal the sick, cleanse the lepers, raise the dead, cast out devils: freely ye have received, freely give* (Matthew 10:7-8)." Have you freely received? If not, it's time that you did. The world, even your family and community needs you now, more than ever. Why watch as those around you continue to get sick and die? Let God anoint you with the Holy Ghost and power to relieve the suffering of those you love. That is why we get saved. It's to save others, rescuing them from every plot of evil against their lives. This is the true power of Kingdom Wealth.

God is using Kingdom Wealth and Power to shake up the darkness of this world. A ***"severe worldwide shaking"*** is in the process. Imagine how people's lives would change if the money and power were in the hands of men and women who love God and love people. Imagine the vast humanitarian efforts that would come forth, without strings attached. Imagine the joy of the masses as the righteous take their positions of authority in the earth. As the Bible says, "*When the righteous are in authority, the people rejoice; but when the wicked beareth rule, the people mourn* (Proverbs 29:2)." People are mourning all over the earth today, but God has heard their cries and has come down with help from above. God is raising up ***"righteous deliverers"*** to comfort all who mourn in these last days.

The devil will try to stop the transfer of wealth and power, but he cannot. There will be turbulence, but God's promises will be fulfilled no matter what that devil attempts. "***It won't be pretty, but it will be necessary,***" says God, ***"for the world to know My Name and witness My power. Darkness will increase, but My Glory will arise even greater in power upon My people." "Do not fear the darkness. It has no power over those who trust in Me. Therefore, whosoever will call upon My Name shall be saved," says the All Powerful, Almighty God.***

Qualifying To Receive Wealth

Earlier we mentioned how Jesus was *"worthy"* to receive for us *"power, and riches, and wisdom, and strength, and honour, and glory, and blessing."* Now let's see how we can qualify to receive all that Jesus bought back for us.

Ecclesiastes 2:26 says, *"For [God] giveth to a man that [is] good in his sight wisdom, and knowledge, and joy: But to the sinner he giveth travail, to gather and to heap up, that he may give to [him that is] good before God."* Heaven is looking for those few *"good"* people who understand that all the wealth of the earth belongs to our Father God. Therefore,

- We don't go after wealth and riches, nor go after our own wisdom (Proverbs 23:4).
- God's wisdom leads to righteousness and justice. It causes us to *"inherit"* wealth and fill our *"treasuries"* (Proverbs 8:20-21).
- When we fear God and delight in His commandments (instruction), wealth and riches will be in our houses (Psalm 112:1, 3).
- The Blessing of the Lord, it maketh rich, and He add no sorrow with it (Proverbs 10:22).

God also has a commandment for the rich: *"Charge*

them that are rich in this world, that they be not high-minded, nor trust in uncertain riches, but in the living God, who giveth us richly all things to enjoy; That they do good, that they be rich in good works, ready to distribute, willing to communicate (I Timothy 6:17-18)." In other words,

- Don't Be Arrogant
- Don't Trust in Riches, Trust in God
- Do Good, Be Rich in "Good Works"
- Be Ready to Distribute
- Be Willing to Share

God is not interested in just making us rich. He wants us to become ***"Amassers and Distributors of Kingdom Wealth."*** God is looking for those who will use the wealth as the Lord wills. ***"Obedience with finances is the money test."*** You must pass ***"the money test"*** to qualify for Kingdom Wealth. God wants to place His people in the ***"billionaire's circle."*** Can He trust you? If so, get ready. God is about to drop the ***"Father lode"*** of wealth and power upon those who will honor Him with their substance. It's not about us. It's about God's global **"Kingdom Mission."** It will take billions and trillions to get it all done. Ask the Lord for specifics about what you must do to receive. Let's *Arise and Shine* for the glory of the Lord!

The Tithe

God's Insurance Policy Against Loss and Death

People think they want wealth until they get it. Then they find out that they have to fight to keep it. With great wealth comes great responsibilities. It means paying greater taxes, greater insurance and banking fees. Having great wealth requires the ongoing services of investment professionals, financial managers and attorneys. Want to buy a mansion? You will need a staff of employees to keep it going. It's no different from being the CEO of a major corporation named YOU, Incorporated.

Then there's the uglier side of having wealth. You become the target of ***"haters and sore losers."*** These are people who enjoy taking from the rich. Some enjoy suing rich people just to see if they can get the money. If you have a nice home or corporate building, they will claim to have fallen and injured themselves. Sell them a product and they will claim that it caused them injury. Drive an expensive car and they will find some way to cause an accident and claim it was your fault. Haters and sore losers will try these things just because they think the wealthy can afford to pay out the big bucks. These people hate you for what you've got. They would never do what is necessary to get wealth legitimately. They are hateful thieves. Plain and simple. Great wealth makes you the target of envious people. It's not the people. It's the devil using people to envy and hate you. "*For wherever there is jealousy (envy) and contention (rivalry and selfish ambition), there will also be confusion (unrest, disharmony, rebellion) and all sorts of evil and vile practices* (James 3:16 AMPC[1])."

Haters will hate, but you must walk in love. Forgive your enemies. Avoid strife and division (racism). These are works of the devil that will block your inheritance. Walk in love and do not fear. Get wisdom instead. It takes wisdom from God to obtain your earthly inheritance. It takes wisdom to keep that inheritance as well. That wisdom begins with the word of God concerning *the tithe*. Jesus came to give us abundant life. It's the thief that comes "*to steal, and to kill and to destroy*" what Jesus gave us (John 10:10). God knew from the beginning how the enemy would

1 "James 3 AMPC." James 3 AMPC - - Bible Gateway, https://www.biblegateway.com/passage/?search=-James%2B3&version=AMPC.

use people to plot to steal from us. That is why He introduced *the tithe.* Look at what happened to Adam and Eve. God told them that they could eat from every tree in the garden, except one. In theory, that one tree was *the tithe.* It was holy (dedicated sacred) to God and it's fruit was not to be eaten. They were tempted by the serpent and ate from the forbidden tree. Adam and Eve fell from the Blessing into the curse, because they disobeyed the commandment of God and touched the holy thing.

By definition, *the tithe* means one tenth. When most people talk about *the tithe,* they are referring to giving 10% of their income to God. Yet, in the Old Testament the Jews were required to *tithe* one tenth of everything they produced on earth. This was a way to prove their dedication and devotion to God. "*And all the tithe of the land, whether of the seed of the land, or of the fruit of the tree, is the LORD'S: it is holy unto the LORD . . . And concerning the tithe of the herd, or of the flock, even of whatsoever passeth under the rod, the tenth shall be holy unto the LORD* (Leviticus 27:30-32)." Tithing was also instituted by the Lord as a way of providing for the Levites (priests) who were not permitted to work because they were solely dedicated to the house of God. *"Bring ye all the tithes into the storehouse, that there may be meat in mine house, and prove me now herewith, saith the LORD of hosts, if I will not open you the windows of heaven, and pour you out a blessing, that [there shall] not [be room] enough [to receive it]* (Malachi 3:10)." Tithes were brought and kept in a storehouse not only for the priest, but also for those in need.

Although there are Christians who argue against it, *the tithe* continues under the New Testament. Our covenant does not require *the tithe*, however, ***"The tithe is a sign of our righteousness."*** Meaning, that righteous people (those who are in right standing with God), will honor Him with their *tithe*. Personally, I have never had a problem with tithing. If the federal government demands taxes for my being in the country, then how could I withhold *the tithe* from the God who put me in earth? *"Render therefore unto Caesar the things which be Caesar's, and unto God the things which be God's* (Luke 20:25)." I also count it an honor to *tithe*. We also honor God with the *"firstfruits"* offering. Firstfruits and tithes are related, but are not necessarily the same. Firstfruits are the *first* of your increase, whether it's a firstborn child, or the first paycheck on a new job, or the proceeds from the first sale in a business. Again, we don't offer firstfruits and tithes out of requirement, but out of love and appreciation to God who has Blessed us with increase. "*Honour the LORD with thy substance, and with the firstfruits of all thine increase: So shall thy barns be filled with plenty, and thy presses shall burst out with new wine* (Proverbs 3:9-10)." Remember, this is an issue of trust. Can God trust us with great substance?

As new covenant believers we don't have to *tithe*, but we don't want to rob God either. "*Will a man rob God? Yet ye have robbed me. But ye say, Wherein have we robbed thee? In tithes and offerings. Ye [are] cursed with a curse: for ye have robbed me, [even] this whole nation* (Malachi 3:8-9)." Robbing God is more than taking money away from Kingdom causes that are dear to the Father's heart. We also rob God by taking away from the Father, the ***"opportunity of protecting"*** what has been given to us. ***"Tithing has the power to protect us against financial loss and death."*** Here is the promise from God to the tither. "*And I will rebuke the devourer for your sakes, and he shall not destroy the fruits of your ground; neither shall your vine cast her fruits before the time in the field, says the Lord* *of hosts* (Malachi 3:11)." The *tithe* will protect the fruit of your labor, the fruit of your body, or anything you produce in this earth. The promise is to "*rebuke the devourer.*" *The tithe* is also powerful insurance against ***"premature death"*** of our children both in and out of the womb. If you love your children and want them to live long on the earth, *tithe*. Then if sickness and death attempts to take them, pull out this scripture and remind the devil that you are a tither. I have used this insurance on many occasions and God has faithfully rebuked that devourer on my behalf.

Finally, there is "*a blessing*" associated with tithing. It's colossal. Tithing provides a supernatural portal, open heavens from which God will release to you solutions for anything you need on earth. This is revelation (supernatural wisdom) from God's throne. The Holy Spirit will reveal schemes and inventions, ***"creative concepts."*** He will provide ways to foil enemy plots against your life. In this way, *the tithe* supplies ***"preventative measures."*** This is ***"Kingdom insurance"*** tithers can count on. People will see this supernatural protection on you, "*and all nations shall call you blessed* (Malachi 3:12)." This is in addition to the Abrahamic Blessing. "*Blessed [shall be] the fruit* *of thy body, and the fruit of thy ground, and the fruit of thy cattle, the increase of thy kine, and the flocks of thy sheep* (Deuteronomy 28:4)." It's God's desire that we increase (multiply) our production in this earth. This is how we dominate. Our obedience to the Voice of the Lord causes us to flourish in the Blessing. "*And the LORD shall make thee plenteous in goods, in the fruit of thy body, and in the fruit of thy cattle, and in the fruit of thy ground, in the land which the LORD sware unto thy fathers to give thee* (Deuteronomy 28:11)." God instituted *the tithe* to protect our *blessings* from thieves and marauders.

Tithing is vital for these last days. We see the devil trying to get people to receive sickness and death with the COVID. He is trying to convince people that law and order are our enemies. God's law behind *the tithe* is our protection and shield. That devil is a liar. His real purpose is to keep us in the curse and death. If he could, that devil would kill every human on earth. Why does he want us out of the way? It has to do with our ***"godly influence."*** Think about it. That devil has almost convinced the world that God wants to spoil their fun. He doesn't want people to know the truth about the goodness of God. Imagine how the world would change if God's kids would began walking in the Blessing. That devil wouldn't be able to touch them. The world is longing for this kind of protection. It can only be found in serving and honoring God with our substance. Think about how many people would flee sex trafficking without fear. Imagine how many homeless people would boldly flee from the streets of our cities, seeking conversion and a Kingdom path to independence. Think about the sick and dying who would clamor for a touch of resurrection power and not only are they raised up, but they go in the power of the Spirit raising others as well. This is evidence that the devil doesn't want the world to see. These are signs and wonders, solid evidence proving that God and Jesus are real. We need this kind of evidence now, more than ever.

For the possessor of Kingdom Wealth *the tithe* is the greatest weapon against the devil. God loved us so much that He offered *His firstfruit* [Jesus] on that cross for us (John 3:16). When God talks about taking back the people, power and wealth of the earth, it equates to the SUM TOTAL VALUE OF JESUS' LIFE AND SACRIFICE. Now, what are you willing to do in this covenant relationship?

Confession Of Faith

It takes great faith to walk in Kingdom Wealth and Dominion. It takes great courage to be able to stand on God's word and face the giants in the land; political giants, religious giants, giants in your own head or even those in your family. To posses the land, we cannot be afraid of the giants who stand between us and our promise land.

These are times that we need to recall what God told Joshua before they took the city of Jericho. *"Moses, My servant is dead* (Joshua 1:2)." New leadership was required to possess the remaining land. What worked in the past would not suffice going forward. A different consecration and anointing was required to endure the **"Kingdom Mission."** Joshua heard God for himself. The Lord gave him specific instructions. *"Now, therefore arise, go . . . every place that the sole of your foot shall tread upon, that have I give unto you . . . As I was with Moses, so I will be with thee: I will not fail thee, nor forsake thee. Be strong and of a good courage* . . . (Joshua 1:2-6)." Under Joshua's leadership, the people expressed a strong determination to follow him. They vowed, "*Whosoever he be that doth rebel against thy commandment, and will not hearken unto thy words in all that thou commandest him, he shall be put to death: only be strong and of a good courage* (Joshua 1:18)." Our faith and determination should put to death every argument that exalts itself against the knowledge of God, and bring every thought under the obedience of Christ (II Corinthians 10:5).

We need to have *great courage* to be able to go in and possess what belongs to us. That courage comes from knowing God's word and developing faith to overcome every challenge. It begins with speaking and meditating on God's word. "*This book of the law shall not depart out of thy mouth; but thou shalt meditate therein day and night, that thou mayest observe to do according to all that is written therein: for then thou shalt make thy way prosperous, and then thou shalt have good success* (Joshua 1:8)."

To receive what God promised, we must believe it in our hearts and confess it with our mouths (Romans 10:9). For years, my pastor Apostle Frederick K.C. Price had our congregation recite a confession at offering time. One particular service, there came a prophetic word saying, ***"as often as you recite this confession, it will bring forth an equal measure of wealth"*** into the lives of the one who recites it. When I heard this word, I got no witness in my spirit that this was for me. So, I filed it away, leaving the door open for the Holy Spirit to minister it to me later. The next morning, I was getting ready for work and the Lord brought to my mind the prophetic word about the confession. I asked if that word was for me. The Lord said, ***"Yes, it is."*** Then I asked, "How often do I need to recite it?" He responded, ***"How much wealth do you want?"*** I began to say, "I want no limits." Before I knew it, the Holy Spirit fell on me and I began reciting the confession numerous times over a forty-five (45) minute period.

The words were flowing out of my spirit at a supernatural rate. I had no idea how many times I repeated that confession. As the anointing of God fell upon me, something was releasing out of my spirit. It was wealth. It began pouring our of me; flowing like a mighty river. To this day, when that wealth flows from my spirit, money is released into my hands within days, minutes and hours. This is supernatural wealth that comes directly from the Kingdom that resides within the spirit of every believer. This is true *prosperity* that is destined for the child of God, for the establishment of the covenant in his or her life.

Below is my recollection of that confession. It is an oath and a commitment to God's covenant based on Deuteronomy 26. The Lord has brought us into a *"good land,"* and has given us the power to get wealth (Deuteronomy 8:18). God and Jesus Christ have completed their part. This confession ensures that we have done our part and that we are now in position to receive the fullness of our covenant promise.

The Confession

Heavenly Father, I am in the land You swore to give me, the Kingdom of Almighty God. I was a sinner serving satan. He was my god. But I called upon the of Jesus and You heard my cry, and delivered from the power of darkness and translated me into the Kingdom of Your Dear Son. Jesus, as My Lord and High Priest, I bring the firstfruits of my income to you so that you can worship the Lord our God with them. Father, I rejoice in all the good you have given to me and my household. I have heard Your voice and have done according to all that You have command me to do. Now, Father, as You look down from your holy habitation from Heaven to bless me according to Your word, I now believe that I receive those Blessings according to Your word. This is my confession of faith in Jesus' Name.

The Restoration Of God's Ancient Kingdom Dynasty

It was about ten years after the Lord taught me about Kingdom Wealth that He also began speaking about "***Restoring His Ancient Kingdom Dynasty***" in the earth. As the Prophet Daniel said, "*And the kingdom and dominion, and the greatness of the kingdom under the whole heaven, shall be given to the people of the saints of the most high . . . Hitherto is the end of the matter* (Daniel 7:27-28)."

I remember what Daniel said about the Kingdom, but I had never heard nor read anything about God's "***Ancient Kingdom Dynasty.***" God isn't just restoring a Kingdom. He is restoring a "***Dynasty,***" which is a lineage of powerful rulers. We, the people of God are "*the saints*" who shall possess the Kingdom. Even now, that Kingdom resides within us (Luke 17:21). We are that "***Dynasty,***" the lineage of powerful leadership that God is restoring in the earth. This amplifies the scripture that says, "*For if by one man's offence death reigned by one, much more they which receive abundance of grace and of the gift of righteousness* *shall reign in life by one, Jesus Christ* (Romans 5:17)." The Lord is calling us to rule and reign in this life. This also gives new meaning to the scripture that says, "*For ye know the grace of our Lord Jesus Christ, that, though he was rich, yet for your sakes he became poor, that ye through his poverty might be rich* (II Corinthians 8:9)."

Beloved, God wants us rich in every way. God is calling His people to reign in this earth. Who will follow us if we have no proof of God's power working in our lives? How can we live like paupers and talk about the riches of our Father's Kingdom? How can we choose to live in a shack on earth and talk about having a mansion in Heaven? If indeed we are heirs of God, then as the Bible says, "*wealth and riches*" should be in our house (Psalm 112:3), not only in Heaven, but also on earth. If we are members of God's Royal family, why haven't we received our earthly inheritances? Even as I write, I hear the Holy Spirit asking again, "*How long [are] ye slack to go to possess the land, Which the LORD God of your fathers hath given you* (Joshua 18:3)?" I also say by the spirit, that God has a people in the land who will go in and possess all that the Father has given them, and they will do so before Jesus returns. God is restoring His Kingdom and every man-made kingdom will be ***"dismantled"*** in these last days. The Prophet Daniel said that God's Kingdom would *"break in pieces and consume"* all other kingdoms (Daniel 2:44). It all shall be restored back to God. In Jesus' Name. Yet, most of us have been taught that Jesus will come back and restore all things. That is not what the scriptures tells us. The prophets taught that the spirit of Elijah would first come and restore all things (Malachi 4:5). Again in the Book of Acts, Peter preached that Jesus would remain in Heaven *"until the restitution of all things* (Acts 3:21)."

Even in our day, people are fearful that the end will come because evil men devise a sinister plot to blow up the world with nuclear war or by unleashing some biological weapon. NOT SO! God will have the final say, not mankind. This is God's earth. Therefore it will be God's plan that will determine how things will end. Let me share what the Holy Spirit revealed to me. I was awaken early one morning hearing, ***"the Kingdom must be delivered up."*** I responded. "Yes, Lord, I know the Kingdom must be delivered up and then the end will come." He repeated again,

"the Kingdom must be delivered up." Okay? This got my attention. I got out of bed and opened my Bible to I Corinthians 15:24. *"Then cometh the end, when he shall have delivered up the kingdom to God, even the Father; when he shall have put down all rule and authority and power."* Then the Holy Spirit began to download spiritual truths that I knew, but had never put them all together. It was like a *light* had gone off in my spirit.

The Lord began reminding me of everything He had said about my assignment in the earth. Inside of my spirit, I heard. ***"We must do it. We are Jesus' Body in the earth. We must take up and finish what He started. The Body of Christ, we go in His Name."*** My spirit was confirming that the Body of Christ is required to ***"deliver up the Kingdom,"*** not Jesus, but the people of God. It is time for his sons and daughters to ***"deliver up the Kingdom."*** Jesus did his part. Now all of heaven is waiting for us to do our part so that Jesus can return. Can we do it? Yes, we can! We've sang songs about going to the enemy's camp and taking back what he stole from us. Now is the time to actually go forth in Jesus' Name and do it. We have a significant part to play in restoring God's earthly Kingdom.

Jesus' death and resurrection was always about restoring ***God's Ancient Kingdom Dynasty*** in the earth. This was God's plan all along. Again, it was never about going to Heaven because according to the Bible, Heaven is coming to earth (Revelation 21:1-2). It was never about the Church, although God has used the Church to spread the gospel in the earth. Most of us were taught that God's Kingdom was all about the Church, but in reality the Kingdom is about every facet of human existence. Let me explain.

Years ago, I had the pleasure of home schooling my neice who was in third grade at the time. In addition to taking an American history course, she was given the opportunity to study the history of other countries as well. She chose to read about Africa and China. As we read through those books, it was interesting to note that ancient dynasties were renown for their legendary wealth and power. The book on China listed every ancient dynasty and the contributions each made to the world. It was phenomenal. As I read, the Lord began speaking to me, ***"Imagine what My Dynasty would look like in ages to come."*** Those words set my imagination on fire. Like those earthly kingdoms, ***God's Kingdom Dynasty*** would leave its mark on government, education, family, arts, entertainment, business and religion. There would be no area of human life that would not be impacted by God's Kingdom. Wasn't that the purpose of the gospel? "*And Jesus came and spake unto them saying, All power is given unto me in heaven and in earth. Go ye therefore, and teach all nations . . . teaching them to observe all things whatsoever I have commanded you* (Matthew 28:18-20)."

In this passage, Jesus gave us His authority to go to all nations; teaching them to obey His commandments. This is a powerful Kingdom mandate, which is much different than just going to Sunday services. This an edict from King Jesus! Mark's gospel contains even stronger language. "*Go ye into all the world, and preach the gospel to every creature. He that believeth and is baptized shall be saved; but he that believeth not shall be damned* (Mark 16:15-16)." Those who don't believed are damned? This is the judgment upon those who reject our King's commands? Yes! Even after His resurrection, Jesus was seen forty-days, "*speaking of things pertaining to the Kingdom of God* (Acts 1:3)." The apostles were ever so mindful that Jesus came to restore God's Kingdom in this earth.

They asked Him, *"Lord, wilt thou at this time restore again the kingdom to Israel* (Acts 1:6)?" Notice that they didn't ask about Heaven. They didn't ask about the establishment of churches. They wanted to know when the Kingdom order would be restored in this earth. And why not? Jesus only taught about the Kingdom. It is the only message He commanded us to preach.

While on earth, Jesus sent out the twelve disciples commanding them, *"And as ye go, preach saying, 'The Kingdom of heaven is at hand.' Heal the sick, cleanse the lepers, raise the dead, cast out devils; freely ye have received, freely give* (Matthew 10: 7-8)." Jesus also sent out the seventy, sending them out two by two into every city, commanding them, *"And heal the sick that are therein, and say unto them, 'The Kingdom of God is come nigh unto you* (Luke 10: 1, 9)." The Lord gave them a warning for those cities that would reject them saying, *"Even the very dust of your city, which cleaveth on us, we do wipe off against you: not withstanding be ye sure of this, that the Kingdom of God is come nigh unto you . . . it shall be more tolerable in that day for Sodom, than for that city* (Luke 10:1-12)." This was strong language of judgment against the cities that rejected the message of the Kingdom. The Lord pronounced judgment upon them all. Throughout the Book of Acts, the first apostles went about preaching the gospel of the Kingdom, even to the uttermost parts of the earth. Judgment fell upon those who came against the Kingdom message. Modern Christianity has greatly rejected the message of the Kingdom. They taught church doctrine. They taught about Heaven and Hell, but not about God's Kingdom. Therefore, the Church at large has been labeled, "non-essential," powerless against the troubles of the world. This is a mockery of our God and His power.

Jesus only taught the Kingdom both in His earthly ministry and after the resurrection. Why didn't the Church do the same? The apostles in the early Church preached the Kingdom. Why didn't the latter Church follow suit? Somewhere along the line, the devil kept the Church in religion where we would never learn of our true identity and power we have been given in Christ. Religion makes men lazy saying, "God is in control." This religious ***"cop-out"*** caused them to ***"opt-out"*** of their Kingdom heritage. To be part of ***God's Kingdom Dynasty***, one must know who they are in Christ. We must believe what God says about us. The Bible says that we have been made *"kings and priests"* unto our God (Revelation 5:10). The Apostle Peter said that we are *"a chosen generation, a royal priesthood an holy nation* (I Peter 2:9)." Indeed, we are sons and daughters (Romans 8:16) of the Most High God, which makes us *"gods"* after the image and likeness of our Father. That also makes us *"heirs of God and joint heirs with Christ* (Romans 8:17)." Like Father Abraham, we are also *"heirs of the world* (Romans 4:13)." The Apostle Paul said, *"Therefore let no man glory in men. For all things are yours* (I Corinthians 3:21)." We have the commission from our Lord. We go into the world with His authority and in His power. The earth is our inheritance (Psalm 2:8). Everything is ours. The Kingdom has been given to us. It's within us. Now is the time to possess that Kingdom in the earth.

This earth was created for the enjoyment of God's family. When Adam sinned, it was all stolen. Babylon [the world system] has been peddling stolen goods ever since Adam fell. The devil's kids want to keep our stuff. They also want position and power, yet the true wealth and power belongs to the sons and daughters of Almighty God. Everything belongs to God's kids. We are the rightful kings and lords of this earth. Adam abdicated his throne to do his own thing. Jesus came, not only as a man, but as the appointed King of God's Kingdom, in order to restore Heaven's ***"kingship"*** back to men on earth. This revelation about ***"The Restoration Of God's Ancient Kingdom Dynasty On Earth"*** has to be one of the most powerful revelations of these last days. We have read about the wealth and power of Queen Esther, of Kings David and Solomon, and that of Joseph. Yet, our generation is about to experience an even ***"greater glory"*** in these final episodes of God's earthly production, that He calls ***"His Grand Finale before Jesus returns."*** The Lord God founded and established this earth for His Eternal Purpose. He will see to that purpose until the very end. His ***Kingdom Dynasty*** will be restored in the earth, before Jesus returns.

It's time for the Body of Christ to arise and take down the kingdom of darkness. This shall be ***"A Battle Royale: The kings of the Kingdom overcoming the kings of the earth."*** Why else would the Lord have taken me to His Armory and to His War Room? We have a battle to win, but we don't war against flesh and blood. We war against, *"principalities, against* *powers, against the rulers of the darkness of this world, against spiritual wickedness in high places* (Ephesians 6:12)." These spirits operate over cities and regions of the land. These same spirits can also operate through governors, mayors and presidents of nations who don't follow after God. When the Holy Spirit called this a ***"A Battle Royale"*** He didn't lie. Our biggest opponents will come from leadership in the high offices of the land, whether in government, the Church or in industry. These are the *"kings"* of the earth that Daniel saw in his visions. He called them *"beasts* (Daniel 7:3,7,12,17)."

The Book of Revelation talks about the *"mark of the beast* (Revelation 16:2)." This is not a physical beast, but a leader of nations who is committed to despotism (tyranny). The beast in our day is the world system that has enslaved human beings under government leadership that opposes God. Nevertheless, everything must be restored, every business, school, government and organization and culture has to be restored back to God, or else Jesus cannot return. Scripture must be fulfilled. That wall map in the War Room showed that God's family is destined to possess everything in this earth, as His Royal Family should.

In order for the ***Kingdom Dynasty*** to be restored, God's people have to take a stand as the rightful heirs of the world. That's a tall order for religious folk who have a *"grasshopper"* mentality. They are like those who refused to go possess the promised land in Moses' day (Numbers 13:33). God was not pleased with them. Neither will He be pleased with those who refuse to possess the land in our day. Time is short. Jesus must return soon. Those who refuse God won't see the wealth or walk in the position as kings of our God. Those who do receive the wealth will have to be ever so mindful to give God the glory for all He has done. *"But thou shalt remember the LORD thy God: for it is he that giveth thee power to get wealth, that he may establish his covenant which he sware unto thy fathers, as it is this day* (Deuteronomy 8:18)."

We are ***Dynastic Rulers*** over our Father's earth. Jesus is the King of kings, and Lord of lords. We, the Body of Christ are the kings and lords over which Jesus reigns. We are a ruling family possessing power in both in Heaven and in earth. It is not by our power that we rule. It is God the Father who endued us with His wealth and power. On our own we can do nothing. We have been anointed and appointed to rule over the earth with the Blessing. As our instructions come from Heaven, we decree the Father's will in the earth. Strict adherence to this basic principle of Kingdom authority causes us to subdue the enemy with great power.

Let me end with a personal revelation. One day I heard these words in my spirit, ***"It's time to take our places in the world. Time to show the world who He [God] is."*** A few days later, I was minding my own business, when lo and behold, *I saw a "watcher" in the realm of the spirit. This demon was seated in the White House watching every move I made in the spirit. This person attempted to block my prayers. He attempted to block my family, my marriage, every promise of God. Then one day this "watcher" saw money coming to me and he stepped in and took it. What happened from this point on was insane. The Lord would have me call forth my money. Every time I called it, my money would turn into a noose around this person's neck. Then one time the Lord had me call forth my money, it split this person's body in half and he fell into hell. This person attempted to come back from hell in the form of a beast to devour my family. I called forth my family and the angels delivered them out of the grip of this* *beast.* Shortly after this spiritual encounter, the Lord showed how the nation was being covered in another level of darkness because of this leader. The battle with this ***"watcher"*** ensued, yet, I remained faithful to God's word in prayer and praise. A couple of weeks after that encounter I had a visitation from the Lord. *I was praying in fierce tongues and went into a praise. Then I saw the Lord, as I appeared to be standing in His Temple. I was wearing a flowing ball gown that had jeweled designs all down the front of it. Over that gown was a luxurious queenly robe. It was red with white fur along the edges of it. The Lord placed a huge crown on my head. It's points were extremely high. With His scepter, the Lord tapped me on the head and shoulders and said,* ***"Rule and Reign in My Name!"*** *Then I walked down the long center aisle of the Temple, escorted by a host of Kingdom military officers on either side. All the hosts of heaven were there. Then I heard,* ***"It's time to go possess the land!"***

"And the Kingdom and Dominion, And the Greatness of the Kingdom Under the Whole Heaven, Shall Be Given to The People of The Saints of The Most High . . . "
" . . . Hitherto is the end of the matter."
Daniel 7:27-28

PRAYER OF SALVATION

ARE YOU READY TO REIGN OVER THE CIRCUMSTANCES OF LIFE?

Begin by **making Jesus the Lord of your life!** Just read the following prayer aloud.

Dear God,

I want Jesus to be Lord over my life. I receive your free gift of righteousness right now. I renounce the devil and sin, and desire to spend the rest of my life serving you. Fill me with your Holy Spirit, and lead me to the your perfect will for my life. I also want to receive an abundance of your grace to fulfill all you would require of me. I ask this all in Jesus' Name. Amen.

IF YOU SAID THIS PRAYER

Welcome To The Family Of God!

- Read the Bible daily
- Ask the Holy Spirit to teach you.
- Do whatever He tells you to do.
- Join a local spirit-filled Bible teaching church

Enjoy Your New Life In Christ!

Made in the USA
Monee, IL
04 November 2026

67379466R00046